Words
FOR
Leycester

Words

FOR

Leycester

Readings for Times of Grief

CAROLINE DEVENISH-MEARES

Library of Congress Control Number:		2022919069
ISBN:	Hardcover	978-1-6698-3239-3
	Softcover	978-1-6698-3238-6
	eBook	978-1-6698-3237-9

Print information available on the last page.

Rev. date: 10/12/2022

To order additional copies of this book, contact:
Xlibris
AU TFN: 1 800 844 927 (Toll Free inside Australia)
AU Local: (02) 8310 8187 (+61 2 8310 8187 from outside Australia)
www.Xlibris.com.au
Orders@Xlibris.com.au
827772

Contents

Dedication

Leycester is my only son, born on 21 March, 1986, with my husband Rochford. He passed from this life on 4th July, 1999 as a result of a single vehicle accident on the Great Northern Highway at the Ord River in The Kimberley in Australia. I was the driver of this vehicle.

Leycester passed at the scene. The rest area is now named after him. My family and I set up a scholarship in his name at Hale School, in Wembley, Western Australia, for a year 8 boarder to have some cricket tuition, a bat, and a camp.

If you would like to contribute to the school scholarship, contact

> Hale School
> 160 Hale Road, Wembley Downs
> Ph- +(61) 08 93479777

Leycester was a shining light amongst our family and friends with his caring nature. He had dreams of playing cricket for Australia. His favourite saying was 'No act of kindness, no matter how small, is ever wasted' by Aesop.

Time to Be Present

As the dawn is breaking
The rising of the sun has just begun
The troubles of yesterday are behind
The day is new
It is time to be present
Feel the wind in your hair
Feel the sun on your back
Taste the flavours of nature's produces
Enjoy the smells of nature's fragrances
The heart will be heavy from loss
The pain will be calling
It is your time to be present
The power of now is with you
Be present in the moment
Look for the positives in your loss
There are gifts our loved ones have left behind
The love they shared
The good times of great experiences they dared
The lessons they gave us
The warmth of their love and friendship
Guidance for the person you are today
They live on in us with their words
The dawn is breaking
The rising of the sun has just begun
It is your time to be present
Time to be present in the moment.

 Going Home

From the beginning of time
I have learnt to walk and talk
I have been taught by the best
I have travelled and had my adventures
I have loved and am loved
I have a strong supportive family
I have had my children
Enjoyed my grandchildren
I have given my all to my community and friends
As I leave you to go home from whence I begun
I am forever grateful to have had you all in my life.
I am going home.

I Dreamed A Dream

One night I dreamed a dream.
I was walking along the beach
Scenes of my life flashed before me
I felt I was there again
As I was walking along the beach
Looking back, I saw footprints
Sometimes there were two sets
Sometimes there was only one set
I didn't understand at first
I said to my Lord
'Your promise was to walk with me always if I followed you'.
Looking back, I saw footprints
There was only one set in the low points in my life
I said to my Lord
'I needed you most at these times. Where were you?'
My Lord replied
'At these low points in your life, you will only see
one set of footprints. This is when I carried you.
Other times the two sets are from you and I as we walked beside each
other'.
One night I dreamed a dream.
You were there, Lord, as you promised to be.

Until We Meet Again

May the road rise to meet you on your journey.
May the stars light up your path.
May the wind always be at your back.
May the sun be warm upon your face.
May the rain fall softly upon your fields.
May the flowers in your garden blossom.
May your troubles be less.
May your blessings be more.
May nothing but happiness come through your door.
May you find all your successes in what you do.
What is for you will never go by you.
Until we meet again,
In those green green fields of old Ireland.
Enjoy your journey.
Set the world on fire,
To light up your path.
Don't let the grass grow under your feet.
What is for you will never go by you.
Until we meet again,
In those green green fields of old Ireland.

The Earthly View

One morning, as I awoke, the sun was shining through the window. I got out of bed and walked towards the window. As I looked out, I saw little children playing on the swings and monkey bars. The playground was brilliantly built and painted. I sat having breakfast when I saw the corn swaying back and forth in the slight breeze. It was harvesting season. I was not surprised that one of the harvesters left the huge shed. It started to rain, and the children ran inside.

After the rain had cleared, the beautiful rainbow appeared in the dark overcast sky.

The harvester was coming back from his daily job while I was having supper. After supper, the sun started to go down, slowly casting a beautiful orange-pink look about the sky. As I was going to bed, I looked out at the full moon shining brightly. All was as it was meant to be.

Leycester Devenish-Meares

Let Love In

You can shed tears that he is gone.
Let love in to lead you to happiness.
It is best not to be in that state of emptiness.
Tears can be shed as he has gone.
You can smile when you hear his favourite song.
Close your eyes, he will not be back.
He will still be with you when you follow that familiar track.
The heart will feel empty as he is not seen.
Reflect back to your memory bank to find where you and he have been.
You can turn back time and live in yesteryears.
This will only bring back your tears.
You can be happy for the time he was here.
In those tomorrows to come, know that he will be near.
Remember him and cherish the memories.
All your times will remain in the pages of your histories.
You can cry, close your mind and feel that emptiness.
It is best for you to smile, open your eyes,
Let love in to lead you to happiness.

Note: Now that the book is yours, the words 'he' can be substituted with 'she' or 'they'.

When Someone Dies

When someone dies (When Leycester passed)
Their (His) body will leave us (you)
We cannot touch them (him) physically
There is a silent magic
They (Leycester) leave (leaves) with us (you)
Their (His) spirit that will have a far greater touch
We (You) will believe they are (he is) our (your) guiding angel
They (He) will be the birds that drop in with their chirping
to say 'hello'
They (He) will be the shadows in the warm sun
that wakes us (you) up and puts us (you) to bed
They (He) will be the winds that turn the wind spinners when there
is stillness
They (He) will be the raindrops on the grass
that refreshes our (your) souls (soul)
They (He) will be the rainbows that splashes
the colour into our (the) skies
They (He) will be the clouds dancing
way up high on those stormy days
They (He) will be the crests on the waves
that tug at our tides

They (He) will be the shooting star
that surprises us (you) while we (you) are waiting
They (He) will be the wind songs whispering back to us (you),
'I am doing fine. I am always with you'.

Note: The book is now yours. You can be personal for someone and
use a name. You can just substitute the 'they' word with 'he' or 'she'.

Let Me Go

I have come to the end of the road
The sun has set for me.
Why cry for my soul that has been set free?
Let me go.
Miss me but not for too long,
Not with your head bowed low.
Remember the times and the love we shared.
Let me go.
This is the journey I must take alone.
Each of us will go it on our own.
This is a step on my journey home.
Let me go.
When you feel lonely and sad at heart,
Turn to your family and friends.
Bury those sorrows by reliving the good times we shared.
Miss me, but let me go.
My time has come.
It is not your time to be glum.
Celebrate, my life has been great.
You can miss me,
Let me go.

I Am Not There

Do not stand at my grave and weep
I am not there, I do not sleep
I am the winds the blow
I am the diamond glints on the snow
I am the sunlight on the ripened grains
I am the gentle autumn rains
I am your shining stars at night
When you wake, I am the morning light
I am the sunset in the west
I watch over you while you rest
I am the clouds above
I live on inside those I love
Do not stand at my grave and weep
I live on in the memories you keep
I am not there, I did not die
I am way up high
I am in the memories you keep
Do not stand at my grave and weep
I am not there.

Love Itself Lives On

Those we love remain with us,
For love itself lives on.
Cherished memories never fade because a
Loved one's gone,
For love itself lives on.
Those we love can never be more than a thought away,
For as long as there is memory, they will live on in our hearts,
For love itself lives on.
We will visit places we shared with our loved ones.
Those memories will be forever strong,
For love itself lives on.
We will hear their special songs,
This will bring back our feelings,
Of joy and gratitude for having them in our lives,
For love itself lives on.

I Wish You

I was sitting at the bus stop. I saw an elderly lady and a younger man. I overheard her say,

'I wish you abundance'.

The young man said, 'I love you for all the things you do for me'. They hugged, and he added, 'I wish you abundance too'. He boarded the bus and left.

She watched the bus leave with tears in her eyes.

I was taken in by the scene and asked the elderly lady if there was anything I could do.

She smiled and thanked me. She said that she was saying goodbye to her only grandson. 'I am close to him, he used to live with me, and now he lives a long way away. He knows that the next time he comes back, it will be for my funeral as I am very sick'.

I said, 'I heard you say, "I wish you abundance". What did that mean?'

She smiled again and said that it was a saying in the family passed down through

the generations.

She closed her eyes and said it from memory.

'I wish you abundance of sun to keep a bright outlook . . . I wish you abundance of rain to value the sun. I wish you abundance of happiness to keep your spirit strong. I wish you abundance of pain to make life's joys precious. I wish you abundance of luck to meet your needs. I wish you abundance of loss to value what you keep. I wish you abundance of hellos to help you through your final goodbye. This is what I wish for you'.

To Everything, There is A Season

To everything there is a season and a time to every purpose under the heaven:

A time to be born and a time to die, a time to plant and a time to pluck up that which is planted;

A time to kill and a time to heal, a time to break down and a time to build up;

A time to weep and a time to laugh, a time to mourn and a time to dance;

A time to cast away stones and a time to gather stones together;

A time to embrace and a time to refrain from embracing;

A time to get and a time to lose, a time to keep and a time to cast away;

A time to rend and a time to sew, a time to keep silence and a time to speak;

A time to love and a time to hate; a time of war and a time of peace.

Ecclesiastes 3:1–8, King James Version

Remember Me

Remember Me.
To the living, I have left
To the sorrowful, I will never be back
To the angry, I was cheated a life
To the happy, I am now at peace
To the faithful, I have never left
I cannot speak, but I can listen
I cannot be seen, but I can be heard
As you stand upon the shore
Gazing at the beautiful sea,
Don't remember we with sadness
As you look in awe at a mighty forest
And its grand majesty,
Don't remember me with tears
Remember me in your heart
Remember all the laughter
We shared throughout the years
In your thoughts and the memories of the
Times we loved, the times we cried
Remember Me
The battles we fought and won
Now I am content, I made you smile
My life was worthwhile
If you always think of me,
I will have never left
I am always with you, morning, noon, and night
Remember Me.

I Look for You, My Son

I miss you every day, but that is nothing new.
I remember your big smiles
I look for you in others.
I remember the warm embraces we had
I look for you in others.
I remember our lady and man kisses
I look for you in others.
I remember your dreams of playing cricket for Australia
I look for you in others.
I remember your ambition to build houses
I look for you in others.
I remember your generous spirit
I look for you in others.
I remember your enjoyment of playing x-box games
I look for you in others.
I remember your love of baking cakes
I look for you in others.
I remember the love you shared with your sisters
I look for you in others.
I remember your independent self sense
I look for you in others.
I remember your adventurous nature
I look for you in others.
I remember your strength to honour your own decisions
I look for you in others.
I miss you every day.
I am so proud to have had you in my life
I look for you in others.
I always felt you were an old soul that walked this earth before me.
I miss you every day.
The years have slipped by.
You have been gone longer than you lived here.
I still miss you every day, my son.

Sweet Memories

Tears will fall like raindrops
On this sad occasion
There will be days
When you doubt your heart.
You can recover
To bring back those sweet memories
Of all the good times
It may be ever so slow
You will feel the sun again
Hear the winds
See the blossoms of new buds
Touch the sands of the oceans
Smell nature's fragrance
Taste life's joys
It helps me in a small way
To send comfort to you
I know you are strong
The flutter of a butterfly
The discovery of a five-cent piece
The appearance of a rainbow
There will be all sorts of triggers
To bring back those sweet memories
Of all the good times
Your loving heart
Will be filled with tears
Tears that fall like raindrops
Wipe those tears and smile again
Enjoy those sweet memories.

Memories of Your Loved One

Memories of your loved one
Will always be with you.
They live on and are not truly done.
Although we live in the midst of ever changing seasons,
Memories of your loved one will give you reasons
That the tender lasting truths of life
Will remain constant throughout your time.
Cherish those memories of your loved one.
They live on and are not truly done.

My Time Has Come

My time has come
I can hear the beat of the drum
The final curtain is drawn
Let my body go.
I am still in your home
Still in your heart
Still in all those familiar places.
My time has come.
Let my body go.
For it is aged and weary
Don't get too teary
I am still in your home
Still in your heart
Still in all those familiar places.
Look and you will find me around.
Don't get so down.
It is just that my time has come
To let my body go.
My time has come.

The Photo Album

Go to that secret place we loved
Take out the photo album from above
Find that comfortable chair
Breathe, relax, and flick back your hair
Go to where we loved in our secret place
Close your eyes and see my face
Take out your phone, play my favourite tune I loved to hear
Close your eyes and you will see me clear
Take a sip of wine, the sparkling white wine
Close your eyes and you will see me fine
Now open those pages in the photo album
Feel me into your heart I come
Check out those pictures of us
We sure had lots of adventures and fuss
Take a moment and pick one of your choice
Close your eyes, you will hear my voice.

All is Well

Death is nothing at all
I have only slipped away into the next room
I am I, and you are you
Whatever we were to each other
That we still are
Call me by my old familiar name
Speak to me in the easy way
Which you always used
Put no difference into your tone
Wear no forced air of solemnity or sorrow
Laugh as we always laughed
At the little jokes we enjoyed together
Play, smile, think of me
Let my name be ever the household word
That it always was
Let it be spoken without the trace of a shadow
I am waiting for you
Somewhere very near, just around the corner
All is well.

Henry Scott Holland

Freedom is Everywhere

Freedom is a funny word.
It comes in many forms.
Everyone has a little,
Even those who are poor.

People who are imprisoned,
Live the life of shame,
Their freedom is limited,
But they only have themselves to blame.

So when you look around you,
Freedom is everywhere.
Even though you may not know it,
I'm sure it will be there.

John A Johnston

Parting of The Waters

The golden streams of friendship
Are linked for time to come,
But only when the chain doth break
Does the water flow beyond.
This strange new love and fondness
Has seeped with in my soul.
A part of me and yet to be,
A stranger welcomed home.
And now
I'm losing . . .
losing . . .
losing you.
How can they drain this very basin,
Their trickling love replenished?
　　　　No, please don't go . . .
　　　　The river flows on . . .
Still, the destined clouds of life passed by
Bearing tidings of relief.
A stream of affection once more did form
From the drops of friendship it released,
A gift from God to quench my thirst
And bathe the wounds of grief.
Our parting, with time, will weather
In the myth of distant years.
And we will flow as one
From whence love begun.

John A Johnston

Those We Hold Most Dear

Those we hold most dear
Never truly leave us.
They live on
As we hold them most dear.
The kindness they showed us,
We hold most dear.
The comfort they shared with us,
We hold most dear.
The love they brought into our lives,
We hold most dear.
The joy they showered on us,
We hold most dear.
The words they left us,
We hold most dear.
The gift of living adventurously,
We hold most dear.
The safe and familiar ways to plot our life journey,
We hold most dear.
They have not truly left us.
We still hold them most dear.

In Your Time of Sorrow

In your time of sorrow
From the past you can borrow
There is an aching in your heart
You don't really want to be apart
You feel your world is collapsing
This is so very taxing
There are no words to explain
The intensity of your pain
In your time of sorrow
Just know there will always be a tomorrow
There will be comfort from someone
Who understands your grief and can bring back that fun
This will be the comfort you need as you grieve
Time for you to believe
All that you shared was real
It is okay to know the loss and really feel
In your time of sorrow
From the past you can borrow
In your tomorrow, things will be more clear
You can now hold those memories most dear
In your time of sorrow
There will always be a tomorrow.

Let The Memories Remain

Tenderly,
may time heal your sorrow.

Gently,
may friends ease your pain.

Softly,
may peace replace heartache.

Tenderly,
let happiness return.

Gently,
let pleasure return.

Softly,
let hopefulness return.

Let the warmest memories remain.
This is our time to have gratitude for time shared.
Let the memories remain.

Life Goes On

Life goes on
It is a journey
We all take different paths
Along the road
Some are here for a short time
Some are here for a long time
We do not know
When the journey will finally end
It is best to make the most
Of the path we have taken
Have laughter, it will lighten your load
Enjoy the travellers you greet
Explore the playgrounds
Learn from the company you keep
Find your peace so you can rest well
On this journey
You will face challenges
Make great decisions
To help your fellow travellers
To have a better place
Be daring with confidence
Make your mark
When your journey finally ends
You will have everlasting peace
And life goes on.

The Lord is My Shepherd

The LORD is my shepherd;
I shall not want,
He maketh me to lie down in green pastures;
He leadeth me beside the still waters.
He restoreth my soul;
He leadeth me in the paths of righteousness for his name's sake.
Yea, though I walk through the valley of the shadow of death,
I will fear no evil:
For thou art with me;
Thy rod and thy staff they comfort me;
Thou preparest a table before me in the presence of mine enemies:
Thou annointest my head with oil;
My cup runneth over.
Surely goodness and mercy shall follow me all the days of my life:
Awnd I will dwell in the house of the LORD forever.

Psalm 23

There is A Way

Like the promise of a rainbow
when the rain has gone away

Like the first new bud of
Spring that tells us
Winter cannot stay.

Like the rising of the sun
indicates the dawning of a new day.

Like the sounds of laughter

Beckon us to shake off those shades of grey.

In the time of tribulation,

Faith will find a way.

The Healing Touch of Time

It may take the healing touch of time
To ease the pain of your loss.
You are not alone.
We hope you will find comfort
And support along the way.
Open up to your family and friends
You will be in their thoughts and concerns.
They do care for you
In these times of hardship.
It may take the healing touch of time
For you to be at peace again.

 Death Cannot Kill

Death cannot kill
That love that never dies
Love once bestowed on earth
Will always live on
The chair maybe empty
But is it really
It was once filled with that someone
That filled your life with love
Death cannot kill
This love of yours
You will nurture it
You will share and spread this love
Love will live on
In the ones you choose
To fill that chair again
Death cannot kill
This great love of yours
Love will give you another life
Open up opportunities
New Beginnings
You will have treasures
From the one that once lived
Death cannot kill
This enduring love of yours
Their spirit is still with you
Sharing and caring
You have reached a higher plane
That will take you through
Your joys and your sorrows
Death cannot kill
A love like yours.

Forever is Too Far to See

Forever is too far to see
from where we stand today.
Loved ones who have
reached a higher view
have found a perfect home
where every sorrow goes away.

There they will wait
to welcome you and me.

Even though they have gone ahead of us
to that Eternal land
We can be sure they have found
a happy place.
Some day in the future
at our own journey's end
we will greet each other gladly
face to face.
For now, forever is too far to see.

May it Help

May it help to know
that family and friends
Will often think of you
not only at this time
But in the days that follow
The months to come
They will be there
To comfort you
To support you
To love you
To guide you
To bring peace back to you
Hope it helps you to know.

A Prayer for Today

Every day I need thee, Lord,
But this day especially.
I need some extra strength to face whatever is to be.
This day more than any day,
I need to feel thee near
To fortify my courage and to overcome my fear.
By myself, I cannot meet the challenge of the hour.
There are times when human creatures need a higher power.
To help us bear what must be borne.
And so,
Dear Lord, I pray,
Hold on to my trembling hand,
And be with me today.

Amen.

Sorry to Hear

I am so very sorry to hear
that you have lost someone so dear
So precious to your heart
that it is difficult to be apart
I know words can't begin
to comfort you about your kin
Please remember
that whenever each other we encumber
You are very much cared about
Do not ever this doubt
Know that you are being kept in my mind
With the deepest care and love of kind
I am so very sorry to hear
that you have lost someone so dear.

Child of Mine

You were just on loan for a little time
For others to love you before you reached your prime
It maybe for months or even years
There is no need for tears or fears
I have found for you parents of the best
Who will treasure and love you as their quest.
I know your time on earth will be brief
But you will leave a treasure trove of memories to ease your family's grief
I promise you that there will be lessons you teach
To all those within your reach
Child of mine, you are on loan
Oh, how I love through your teachings, others have grown
I have looked this wide world over for students true
The gifts you leave your parents is your cue
To depart from this earthly place
You will be here with the angels to chase
There is no time for bitter grief, I have plans
You are now the guiding light of your clans
Child of mine, you were on loan
You did me proud, bringing all that happiness to those you have known.

Freedom

FREEDOM is the most sought after dream of mankind. It is about having the ability to do whatever you want to do whenever, wherever, and however.

RECOGNITION is the way to show appreciation to others who have helped you on this journey or even shared their time, love, and skills with you for you to be the person you are today.

You will be surprised what is returned to you when you take this position for recognising gratitude in your life.

EXERCISE is the key to a good healthy body to do what you want when you want, where,

and how you want. Exercise submission and be on good terms with all people. Speak your truth quietly and clearly. Listen, not to respond, you will be amazed at what you learn.

Avoid loud, aggressive people to exercise your right to peace. Surrender gracefully to the things of youth.

EMOTIONS are wonderful expressions of you. Be your authentic self. Show vulnerability.

These are essential for you to speak your truth. Nurture your strength of spirit to shield you in misfortunes that may come your way.

DISENCHANTMENT will visit when something or someone is no longer good or worthwhile.

Do not distress yourself. You are a child of the universe. You have the right to be here as does every other living thing. The universe will envelop you, and life will unfold as it should be. Trust in yourself.

OPPORTUNITY will knock in the noisy confusion of life. Take time to evaluate and do it for all the right reasons for you. Don't take too long. Reach for the stars. Strive to be happy to fulfil your dream of freedom.

MEMORIES remind us that nothing lasts forever. Time is ever so precious and should not be wasted. Recognise your achievements. Exercise. Show your emotions. Don't fall victim to disenchantment. Take opportunities and build that memory bank to draw on to enjoy your freedom.

Thank You

What can I say in times such as these?

All I can think of is what should be said and what is known,

In which I offer thanks to you, my friend.

Thank you for the love you give your mother Caroline, for with you,

her love ever lives on.

Thank you for the love you give your father Roch, for with you and your memory, his strength is ever strong.

Thank you for the love you give your big sister Rachel, for the times with you shared are never lost, only revived through memory.

Thank you for the love you give your little sister Ranin, her love for you was ever seen,

and with that, she will grow stronger than all.

Thank you for the friendship you give my brother Cody, the things you shared together are things only known by true friends.

Thank you for the friendship you give my parents Lorraine and Jamie. Having you in our world was only short, but you in our hearts will last forever.

And thank you for the friendship you give me, for without it, I would not know how to laugh.

Simple words by a simple person, but words all true, and all known.

Love you, mate.

Wade Savage

At This Moment

At this moment in your lifetime
You may feel that you are alone
And that loss is something
No one else has ever known
There are those who sympathise
Who know and understand
How much you need
A word of cheer
A smile, An understanding hand
So may it comfort you to know
At this moment in time
That thoughts from others are with you.
You are not really alone
For you have friends and family fair
Who really care.

Stars, I Have Seen Them Fall

Stars, I have seen them fall,
But when they drop and die,
No star is lost at all
From all the star-sown sky.
The toil of all that be
Helps not the primal fault; it rains into the sea,
And still, the sea is salt.

A E Housman

To an Athlete Dying Young

The time you won your town the race,
We chaired you through the market place;
Man and boy stood cheering by,
And home we brought you shoulder-high.

Today, the road all runners come,
Shoulder-high we bring you home,
And set you at your threshold down,
Townsman of a stiller town.

Smart lad, to slip betimes away,
From fields where glory does not stay,
And early though the laurel grows,
It withers quicker than the rose.

So set before its echoes fade,
The fleet foot on the sill of shade,
And hold to the low lintel up
The still-defended challenge cup.

—A E Housman

Rolling with The Times

Rolling with the times,
The answer to the question.
Change has arrived
Not sure what.
Could be the loss of a job.
Could be the breakdown of a relationship.
Could be the loss of a loved one.
Could be the loss of yesteryear with a partner.
Could be an illness.
Rolling with the times,
It is the answer.
There will be another job in the wings.
Believe in your strengths.
There will be another person
With more appreciation of you.
The loved ones have never really left.
They live on in their words and gifts.
The loss of yesteryear opens up
New opportunities to develop new ways.
The illness is a sign to embrace
More about you to survive.
Rolling with the times,
It is the answer to the question
'How are you?'

Lean on Those that Care

Life is full of obstacles
Sometimes they seem so great
That we don't know if we have
The courage and strength to deal with this
Just know
There are family and friends
There are professional people
That are there for you to lean on
They will care for you.
They will build your strength and courage
Restore your faith
They are there for you, for you to lean on
Life obstacles won't seem so great
When you have all this support
My hope for you is to lean on
Those that care
Whenever you need to.

Others Care

It feels there is so little one can say,
So little one can do,
When you have lost a loved one.
We wish we could wave that
Magic Wand
And bring him back to you.
What we can say
To brighten your day.
In a message of sympathy
We want to let you know
Others care.
We also share your loss.
We are here for you to lean on.
We will not be gone.
We are here
Because we care for you.
Maybe this is not so little
That we can do for you
Because we, are the others that care.

The book is yours – him can be substituted with her or they

I Have No Words

I do not know how you feel
I cannot take away your pain
I cannot advise you
I have no words for you
I cannot tell you that you will get over it
Life goes on, and the hurt will still be there
I cannot tell you that you are young to have another child
I cannot tell you that the other children will comfort you
Life goes on, and he will be missed
I do not know how you feel
I cannot take away your pain
I will not tell you to pull yourself together
I have no words for you
I am here anytime you want to talk
I will listen about your loved one
I will laugh with you about all the good memories
I have no words for you
I do not know how you feel
In the time we share
I might learn a little of what you are going through
I hope you feel comfortable with me
And maybe your burden will ease
I have no words for you
Just my time.

Feelings of Love

Feelings of love I send to you.
There will be dark days ahead
And you wish too that you had fled.
Those dark days ahead
Do not dread.
There will be light,
And those dark days will be out of sight.
Feeling of love I send to you.
Strength to face it all,
Will in time call.
There will be light,
And those dark days will be out of sight.
Feelings of love I send to you.
Peace has come to your loved one.
Your sad times are done.
Your faith, love and hope,
Those dark days with them you cope.
Feelings of love I send to you.
You are in my prayers.
For you, there will be another love that cares.
You are in my heart.
We are never far apart.
Feelings of love I send to you.

We Care

We care but do not
Know your sorrow.
We can only express
Our sympathy for your loss.
We are gifting you
Our thoughts and prayers
To comfort you.
If there is anything
That we can do for you,
All you have to do
Is let us know.
We are here to comfort you.
We care for you.

A New Start

Beyond this night of grief and pain,
There will be the sweet realisation of life's gain.
You will see the glimmer of new hope
Is the opportunity to set up a new life scope.
Believe faith will lead the way
To a brighter better day.
You will not know what the future may hold.
Fight for what you believe in, be bold.
Love yourself and always move forward with gratitude in your heart.
Beyond this night of grief and pain, behold, for you, a new start.

He is The Light

He is the Light that brightens
Our paths when it is dark.
He knows our fears that crowd our hearts.
He cares and wants to ignite that spark
To take us through these difficult times
To find peace that will flow to our hearts.
He is the Light that brightens
Our paths when it is dark.
His intention is to bring comfort, joy and hope.
He cares and wants to reignite that spark
To lift us from this heavy yoke
To reduce the burdens in the sorrowful times
To find the love that will fill our hearts
He is the Light.

The Little Prince

'I'm going home today, back to my star to look after the things I love', said the Little Prince. 'But I cannot take this body with me. It's too heavy, and it's too far away'.

The Little Prince took my hand. 'Don't be sad when you see my body, for it is not me. It will be like an empty shell, and there's nothing sad about empty shells. I will be living on my star, laughing on my star'.

'When you look at the stars at night, it will be as if all the stars are laughing. And once you've got over it, you will feel like laughing with me. But you won't know which star is mine, so you'll love looking at all the stars, all 500 million of them. They'll all be your friends'.

Adapted from *The Little Prince* by Antoine de Saint-Exupery

This was a piece in Leycester's school books.

He is Our Hope

We seek to know His will
It seems that it eludes us till
Our anxious pounding heart
Turns to find from the start
His loving arms were always open wide
To all who came to rest inside.

He is our hope
To give us the strength to cope
While our hearts are screaming out for peace
We want this noise to cease
Into His loving arms, we can fall
He is our hope when we call.

I Pray for You

I pray for you
In your time of need
Even though I am
Thousands of miles away
I want you to know
You are in my prayers
I wish upon the stars
That I am there
To comfort you
This is as much as I can do
I pray for you every day
I cannot be there with you
Know I am sending
My thoughts and energies
To support you in your time of need
I pray for you.

Right Now, Be Happy

There is no time like the present
Right now, be happy.
Don't wait until you find love
Right now, be happy.
Don't wait until you find the perfect house
Right now, be happy.
Don't wait until the kids leave home
Right now, be happy.
Don't wait for the vacation
Right now, be happy.
Don't wait until you get a better car
Right now, be happy.
Don't wait until you retire
Right now, be happy.
The truth is there is no better time
To be happy than right now.
Life will be filled with challenges
It is best to be happy right now.
You will have obstacles in your travels
It is best to be happy right now.
There will be unfinished business with associates
It is best to be happy right now.
There will be disenchantment along the way
It is best to be happy right now.
There will be the pain of loss
It is best to be happy right now.
Arguments and disagreements are all part of family life
It is best to be happy right now.
There is no time like the present
Right now, to be happy.
Treasure every moment you have
Right now, be happy.

Treasure your time with that special someone
Right now, be happy.
Learn from your school pals and work colleagues
Right now, be happy.
Enjoy the seasons of nature, summer, winter, spring and autumn
Right now, be happy.
Enjoy the weekend adventures
Right now, be happy.
When retirement comes
Right now, be happy.
Stop waiting.
There is no better time
Than right now to be happy.

Mollie Told Me So

Mollie is my mother. She has a way with words, very brief and straight to the point.

These were her rules for when I was growing up:

1. You only have one life, make it count and make your mark.
2. Whatever you do, do well to the best of your ability.
3. Always put your best foot forward and be kind and considerate.
4. There is no such thing as failures or mistakes. What ever you do will be a learning experience.
5. Make sure your decisions are for the right reason in the given time you have and it stays there.
6. Treat people the way you want to be treated.
7. Do not lie. Always be honest with yourself and others.
8. If you make a commitment, honour it as there is no alternative.
9. Enjoy life, take opportunities, and have no regrets.
10. Be your own person and own what you do.

Goodbye, My Young Friend

There is an aching deep inside me
No strength despite the muscle.
The news so tragic!
Emotions in a twisting tussle.

So young, so burning bright, so cheeky
Too briefly here for us to share.
No more I'll have the chance to tell him,
He is special—just not fair!

The grief, the tears, so many hurting
Our tiny chapel bursts it's seams.
A moving tribute in a sombre service,
The young friend will live on in our dreams.

Our wounded hearts, with time, are healing.
Moving on with sad regret
But strengthened with the memory lasting
Of his touch, we shan't forget.

Printed in Australia
AUHW021518251122
371765AU00004B/4

9 781669 832386